I Québec

*I*t is our pleasure to introduce you to Quebec City, in this first volume of our new series entitled, **Focus**. We feel that you will share our enthusiasm for this exceptional city, the capital of French North America. We hope to provide you with a fresh look at the city through a historical and a contemporary vision.

Our writers, who all have a special love for the city, will accompany you along the way, describing the many facets of Quebec City, while visual artists such as Luc-Antoine Couturier capture the sights and put them into focus.

Enjoy your visit to Quebec City.

Editor
Sylvain Harvey

Photographer
Luc-Antoine Couturier

Greater Québec Area Tourism and Convention Bureau, Parcs Canada, Tourisme Québec, L'Imagier, Michel Harvey, Jean Sylvain, La revue Cap-aux-Diamants

Contributors
Paul Dumont, Christine Risi, Ève Lacombe, Danielle Bertrand, Gérald Boudreau

Graphic Design and Computer Graphics
Marois Conception visuelle • marketing, Deneault Visuel, Larochelle et associés

Consultation and revision
Greater Québec Area Tourism and Convention Bureau, La revue Cap-aux-Diamants, Les visites culturelles Baillairgé inc.

Translation
Rédaction anglaise enr.

Printed in CANADA

We would like to acknowledge all those who through their encouragement and cooperation contributed to this edition as well as SODEC for its contribution under the publication assistance program.

ÉDITIONS
SYLVAIN HARVEY

Toll-free :   1 800 476-2068   (Canada and U.S.A.)
Phone :   (418) 692-1336   (Quebec City area and other countries)
Fax :   (418) 527-2632
E-mail :   sharvey@mediom.qc.ca

Available in :   ENGLISH   ITALIAN
                     FRENCH   GERMAN
                     JAPANESE   SPANISH
                     PORTUGUESE CHINESE

TABLE OF CONTENTS

Legal deposit : 3rd trimester 2001
National Library of Quebec / National Library of Canada

Original Title : Histoire de voir, Québec © 1994, Éditions Sylvain Harvey

Focus, Québec © 1994, Éditions Sylvain Harvey
ISBN 2-921703-44-0 (Second edition, 2001)
Third printing, 2005

Pages 4 and 5 : Quebec : The colorful landscape of Quebec City, fashioned through the ages by Nature, has been inhabited for millennia.

Quebec City, a maritime tradition.

A City Favored by Nature

Quebec City is one of the most beautiful cities in the world and owes much of its beauty to the magnificence of its site. Just to the north are the Laurentians, the oldest mountain chain on the planet. To the south, the more recent Appalachians. Perched high on a cliff, the old fortified city looks down on the Saint Lawrence, one of the world's great rivers. Quebec City is set on a magnificent promontory that dominates a narrow stretch of the river which, after the fertile Ile d'Orléans, opens up into the vast estuary of the Saint Lawrence leading to the ocean. Softening the impact of this dramatic scenery, the Saint-Charles River meanders lazily down to the Saint Lawrence.

The Saint Lawrence River from the Ile d'Orléans to the Beaupré coast. Unchanged for thousands of years.

The power of Nature is evident even at the foot of the promontory on which the city is built.

◄ *The snow geese always return to Quebec City.*

While Nature was generous, it was not in a hurry. During the last Ice Age, the site at Quebec City was covered by a glacier hundreds of meters thick. As the glaciers retreated, the waters of the Gulf of Saint Lawrence flowed past the site and covered the surrounding low-lying land.

The area, covered by the Champlain Sea, waited patiently, deep under water, ready to reveal its beauty and surroundings to the world.

The Quebec City area in the 16th century

The Island Cliff

As the Champlain Sea gradually retreated, the celebrated Cape Diamond, Cap-aux-Diamants, emerged from the water. Several centuries later, a very brief period of time for Nature, the site of Quebec City became an island with tall cliffs protecting it from the sea.

And Nature continued to fashion the site. As the sea retreated, the land so recently freed of the glacier's great weight, began to rise. It blocked the sea to the east and led to the gradual emergence of what is now the upper town. To the west, while the waters were retreating and the land rising, the river settled into a corridor that gradually became what we now call the Saint Lawrence River.

As the climate became increasingly temperate, plant life became richer. This environment was ideal for the arrival and growth of species such as caribou, moose, black bear and beaver. New species such as snow geese, barnacle geese and many kinds of ducks joined the birds already present.

The outlines of this natural environment took shape about 3000 years ago. It is hard to imagine a more impressive setting for the city. Nature had sketched a masterpiece that sat waiting for man to bring to completion.

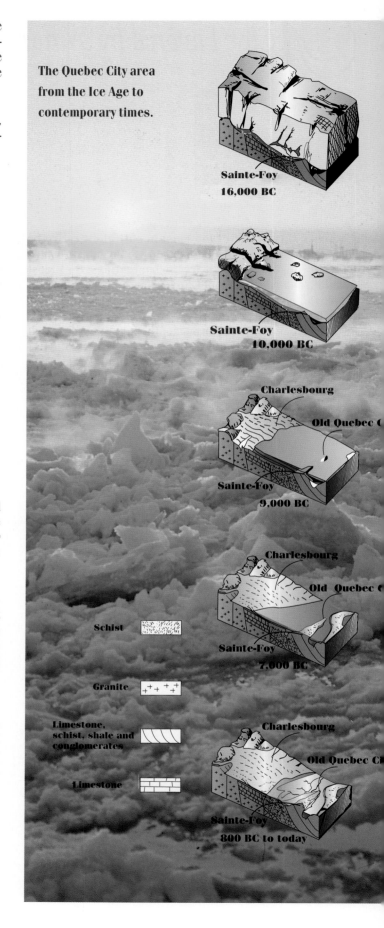

The Quebec City area from the Ice Age to contemporary times.

Sainte-Foy
16,000 BC

Sainte-Foy
10,000 BC

Charlesbourg

Old Quebec C

Sainte-Foy
9,000 BC

Charlesbourg

Old Quebec C

Schist

Sainte-Foy
7,000 BC

Granite

Limestone, schist, shale and conglomerates

Charlesbourg

Old Quebec Ci

Limestone

Sainte-Foy
800 BC to today

Ten Thousand Years of History

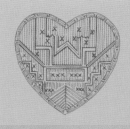

It is surprising how we tend to date the history of the Americas from the arrival of the first European explorers: the Spanish and Portuguese in the South, the English and French in the North, as if only written cultures were significant and had built a civilization. Fortunately, today specialists in geology, ethnography and archaeology assist historians by providing perspective to the outline of history.

Their research places the first human settlements on the site of Quebec City about ten thousand years ago. During that period, the paleo-Indian era, nomadic tribes could easily have reached the Québec promontory, then an island, to hunt caribou. They were the descendants of Asians who began migrating to the Americas over 25 000 years ago when Siberia and Alaska were linked.

These peoples adapted to the varied environments of the new land and over time developed different languages and systems of government.

Parcs Canada / J. Beardsell

Aboriginal communities proudly maintain their traditions today.

Parcs Canada / H. Boucher

Reconstruction of an Iroquois longhouse similar to those seen by Jacques Cartier.

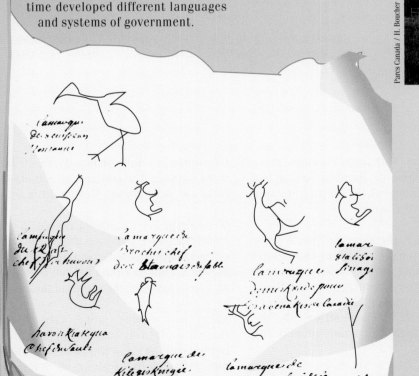

Peace treaty, 1701

When Champlain landed at the site of Quebec City on July 3, 1608 he described the point under Cape Diamond as ideal for the "Habitation" that he would build.

They were nomadic, traveling as their needs required, living in small camps preferably near water. Hunting, fishing and gathering provided their nourishment. As their population increased, they settled in specific areas.

It is estimated that when French navigator Jacques Cartier first explored the area in 1535, a population of about 5000 aboriginals lived along the Saint Lawrence valley. Members of the Iroquois community, they lived next to the Saint Lawrence between Stadacona (Quebec City) and Hochelaga (Montréal). There were probably a dozen settlements, the largest of which were Hochelaga (1500 individuals) and Stadacona (500 individuals).

Stadacona was an important aboriginal trade center and the capital of a region called Kanata. An aboriginal term meaning village or small community, this is the likely origin of the word Canada. The territory of Kanata included areas for a large distance around Metropolitan Quebec City.

When Samuel de Champlain arrived 75 years later, this village had disappeared. The vague, unspecific description that Jacques Cartier had given for its location put it most likely at the foot of the cliff. A later location has not been discovered, although it was probably along the shores of the Saint Charles River.

Today, just outside Quebec City on the Wendake Reserve there is a relatively homogenous and prosperous 1200-member band of the great Huron nation. This aboriginal community, although living alongside a European-based culture, has maintained its own community and culture. Traditional artisans sell their work in the Huron Village.

The Cradle Of French North America

From its former title, Cradle of New France to the current title, la Vieille Capitale (the Old Capital), one thing has remained constant in the heritage of Quebec City: it has always been the heart and soul of the French fact in North America. From all over Québec, and from Acadia, Canada, and the United States, people of French heritage return to be immersed in French history and culture. Even visitors from Europe find it a little like home. For those who want to learn about French culture, Quebec City is the ideal place to begin.

This French fact of Quebec City is due as much to its origins as to its development, its religion and the character and political efforts of its inhabitants. When Champlain founded Quebec City in 1608 following Jacques Cartier's instructions, it was intended to be a center for the fur trade. Its location made it the obvious choice. Quebec City became the main trading point for the new colony and the gateway to the North American continent.

The Catholic Church, in its desire to propagate its faith, sent priests for the colonists and missionaries to convert the aboriginal inhabitants of the New World. The coureurs des bois seeking furs, the missionaries seeking souls and the explorers seeking a passage to China or India established the French fact in the Great Lakes area, then in the very heart of North America and even as far as the Gulf of Mexico. The names of the cities of Detroit, Saint Louis, New Orleans and many more are living proof of these travels.

Tourisme Québec

High over the glow of Place Royale, the Champlain Monument commemorates the founder of Quebec City.

Statues of famous individuals are reminders of an illustrious past.

By the mid-18th century Quebec City had become the capital of a vast territory that occupied two-thirds of North America stretching from Acadia to the Rocky Mountains, and from Hudson Bay through the Great Lakes to Louisiana. The diocese based in Quebec City stretched across the continent, making it the largest diocese in the world.

After the British conquest in 1759, immigrants from England, Scotland and Ireland greatly outnumbered immigrants from France. The local French inhabitants, abandoned by the French nobility, held on to their land, religion and language with determination. Although during the French period of colonization no more than 10 000 immigrants arrived, their descendants throughout North America now number over 12 million.

Education in Quebec City played an important role in maintaining French culture in North America. In 1635, the Jesuits set up a classical college modelled on their French institutions. Then in 1663, François de Laval, the first bishop of Québec, founded the Québec Seminary that became Laval University in 1852. Today it plays a major role in maintaining French culture in America.

With British rule, Quebec City, the capital of an immense French colonial empire, became for a time the center of a British colony. However, revolt in the American colonies and American Independence, along with the arrival in Canada of American loyalists, forever transformed the political landscape. With the division of the country under the Constitution

The Parliament Building in Quebec City is one of the finest public buildings constructed in a French classical style in North America. Its facade incorporates many sculpted figures and coats of arms commemorating the history of the land.

Act of 1791, Quebec City became the capital of Lower Canada and after Confederation in 1867, a provincial capital.

From that time on, Quebec City has always defended the culture and the rights of French civilization that are so strongly rooted in North America.

The steep roofs in Place Royale show how the first Europeans adapted to the harsh winters in Québec.

A view of Quebec City during the French Regime. From the earliest times of the French colony the Vieille Capitale has been an inspiration to artists.

The Only Fortified City in North America

Parcs Canada / J. Beardsell

The Citadel, high on the hill, dominates the strait.

If the old part of Quebec City reminds visitors of the Middle Ages, which go back well before Champlain founded the city, this is due first to its location high on a cliff. It is also due to a refined aristocratic Irishman, Lord Dufferin, Governor General in 1872, whose name is commemorated on the Dufferin Terrace. Dufferin became indignant upon his arrival in Quebec City when he saw the city walls and gates being destroyed. For the sake of progress, a city engineer, Charles Baillargé had undertaken demolition of the walls in line with Hausmann's modernization of Paris.

Vandals and Goths was what the new governor, in a letter to the Secretary of State for the Colonies, called those engaged in tearing down the walls. He brought in the Irish architect William Lynn to draw up new plans for gates inspired by the military architecture of the Middle Ages. Baillargé himself later became associated with these new plans. Quebec City's unique character, a fortified city for centuries, had come very close to being destroyed.

Right from its origins, the first "Habitation" built by Champlain in 1608 brought to mind a medieval castle since it incorporated residential quarters, a storehouse and a military tower with walls raised for its defense. British threats beginning in 1690 led to construction of an incomplete and rudimentary system of defense, that took advantage of natural features in the terrain.

Place Royale is one of the oldest urban sites in the North American continent. Its narrow streets evoke four centuries of history.

Reminders of battles past.

A walk along the fortifications circling the city is an experience unequaled anywhere else in North America.

This was but the first in a series of walled fortifications encircling the city until the British Conquest. The last walls, made of masonry in 1745 by the French, did not play a role in the city's fall in 1759 since the battle took place outside the city.

After the Conquest, the British, while no longer expecting an attack from France, did undertake construction of defensive works in fear of an American invasion as well as a possible uprising by the French population which was more numerous than the English population at the time. They built a citadel and network of Martello towers that can still be seen today.

But it wasn't until 1832 that the fortification system as we know it, including the citadel, was completed. At that time a quarter of the city's space was taken up with defense activities and 25% of the population were soldiers.

With the departure of the British garrison in 1871, the walls were abandoned and some of the military gates demolished, leaving only a semblance of military activity inside the citadel.

Over the years there were several campaigns for modernization and economic progress aimed at demolishing the fortifications. However, defenders of the city's integrity finally won out and now not a year passes without some maintenance or reconstruction work on the fortifications.

As a result, today Quebec City stands on top of the cliff protected by four kilometers, a full two and a half miles, of walls bearing witness to a proud past. It is possible to walk along the top of the walls and scan the horizon, as if for the enemies of old.

The first gates were built to control access to the walled city. The city gates today beckon visitors to enter the Old City ... or to take shelter !

The desire to protect its historic past earned Quebec City recognition as a World Heritage Site by UNESCO.

A Coveted City

The Notre-Dame de la Victoire church after the bombardment of 1759. Rendering of an engraving by A. Benoist after a drawing by Richard Short.

Despite its romantic charm, Quebec City with its fortifications, citadel and cannons commanding the river from the cape retains the dramatic image of strength that allowed it to survive intact. A strategic site and gateway, it was always a coveted military prize.

Only twenty years after it was founded, the Kirk brothers led the first British attack. Victorious, they chased out Champlain and occupied the city until 1632 leaving only destruction in their wake. On his return, Champlain had to rebuild the city.

In 1690, the governor, Louis de Buade, Count of Frontenac, greeted the invading Admiral William Phips with cannonfire, forcing him to return home empty-handed.

It was the arrival of British General James Wolfe in 1759 that changed the tide of history. In the battle on the Plains of Abraham against Montcalm, defender of the city, he was victorious and brought English domination to the colony. The Treaty of Paris in 1763 made New France a British colony.

But, in 1774, fearing the Americans who had just taken up arms to fight for independence, the British lightened restrictive measures on French Canadians. It brought results. Canadians fighting under Governor Guy Carleton were able to fight off the attack against Quebec City by American Generals Richard Montgomery and Benedict Arnold in 1775. Quebec City had nearly fallen into American hands.

The cannons protecting the city are silent. There are still 198 cannons, installed mainly around the perimeter of Cap-aux Diamants.

A frosty fall morning on the Dufferin Terrace in front of the Château Frontenac.

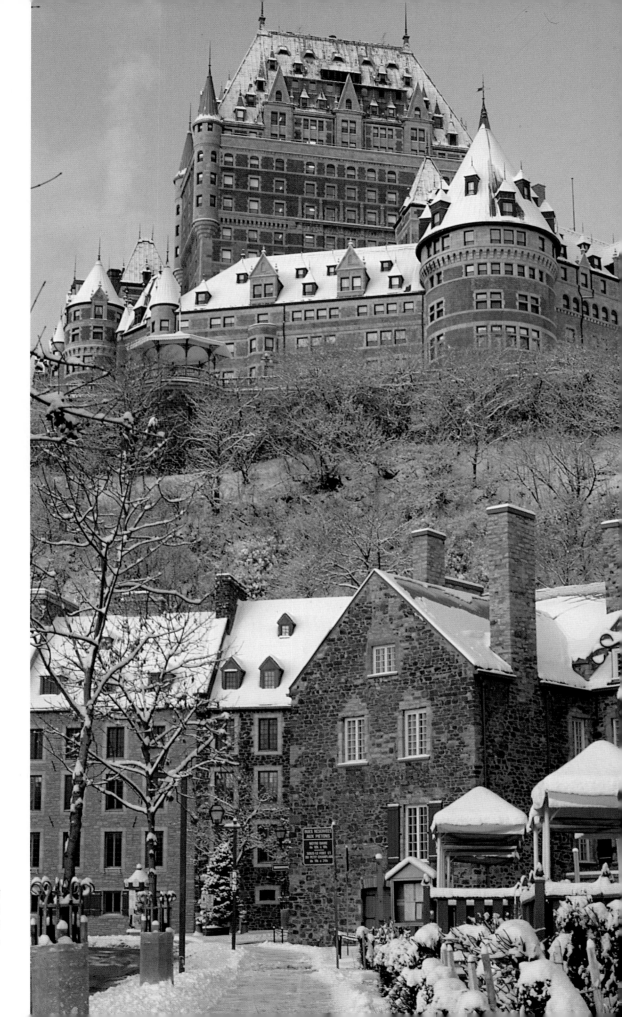

Rising high over Cap-aux Diamants, the Château Frontenac evokes medieval times.

The city founded by Champlain: a meeting place for land and sea, old and new.

The Mighty Saint Lawrence

Quebec City owes its origins and its name to the river. It cannot be separated from the river on which its fate has always depended and on which its vitality still depends.

The city takes its name from the straits next to the city that the Algonquins called Kebec. Some 18 kilometers or nearly a dozen miles wide east of the Ile d'Orleans, the river narrows to a little more than half a mile or one kilometer at Quebec City. For the aboriginals, the Saint Lawrence is the river that walks, while the Europeans described it as the mighty river. Jacques Cartier baptized it the Saint Lawrence and very soon it was known as the mighty Saint Lawrence.

Bustling activity on the river inspired nineteenth century artists. A sketch by Captain B. Beaujoy (1840).

As dreams drift by...

The only way to truly appreciate the splendor of Quebec City is from the Saint Lawrence River.

The ice bridge between Lévis and Quebec City in 1892.

The Saint Lawrence is the longest river navigable by ocean-going ships. Near Quebec City, 1300 kilometers (or about 800 miles) from the Atlantic, it is still salty and the tides against city docks can reach seven meters (22 feet). Here the current reverses direction, providing a surprising spectacle in winter as ice floes move back and forth in front of the city. The river makes Quebec City an inland seaport. Until 1735 when the first network of roads linked it to Montréal, the river was the only travel and trade link between the two cities.

Under the French Regime in the first half of the 18th century, the port handled dozens of ships every year that brought goods, colonists and travelers while picking up cargo composed mostly of fur pelts. A section of the port was used for shipbuilding and repairs.

After the Conquest, British merchants arrived setting up warehouses and building wharves. There was a lucrative export trade in timber to England along with imports of merchandise. Port activities increased to the point that in the mid-19th century there were 1200 ships per year sailing the Saint Lawrence. During that period more than a million immigrants from England, Scotland and Ireland arrived, many on their way to the United States or other parts of Canada. Others would stay.

At that time and right up to the end of the 19th century, the river was not navigable in winter. But winter brought a joyous spectacle when the shores at Lévis and Quebec City were linked by an ice bridge lined with spruce trees set in the ice. Travelers could stop at refreshment stalls during the crossing. There were horse races, skating and horse-drawn sleigh excursions.

When the railroad was built, the Port of Quebec City became a major grain and paper exporting center, but went into decline when the seaway opened and Montréal and American ports expanded. However with port modernization, this situation is being reversed and Quebec City remains a very active trade center based on the port and its river.

In summer, residents along the Saint Lawrence use it for recreation. A marina has recently been installed in the Louise Basin and every day hundreds of amateur skippers sail out onto the river, maintaining a seagoing and navigating heritage. Thousands of visitors on seagoing cruise ships land only a few steps from Place Royale.

The Old Port, which is now separate from the commercial port, has become popular with residents and tourists who stroll along the riverfront. For those who want to discover the islands downriver or enjoy the panoramic sights, cruise ships depart regularly.

In times past, winter ice halted traffic on the Saint Lawrence, but now it is kept open for navigation all year round.

Contemporary Beauty And The Charm Of Tradition

Nature has fashioned a magnificent site at Quebec City and civilization has developed it well. Throughout its history, the residents of Quebec City have taken advantage of the natural beauty of the site, developing it with art and taste, beautifying it, improving it and ensuring that its historic charm is maintained.

The roads up the cape are named imaginatively: Côte de la Montagne, Côte du Palais, Côte de la Canoterie and Côte d'Abraham. It is surprisingly enjoyable, despite the climb, to follow the unpredictable curves and corners, stopping to contemplate the landscape that changes at every step. The most hidden and beautiful may be the Côte Gilmour that winds its way through majestic elms and maples up to the Plains of Abraham.

The discoveries are only beginning. Once inside the city walls, the streets intersect at all angles or head off up or down in every direction from small squares or parks. Nothing is level or at right angles. The capricious terrain leads the way as if trying to make visitors lose their way.

Petit Champlain street is the heart of the oldest commercial district in North America. Designer clothes, jewelry and art objects made by the artists and artisans who live in the neighborhood can be found in its many boutiques.

Multi-paned windows and closely-nestled houses help give Quebec City its European character.

The street names are a treasured link with history. Des Jardins street, for example, refers to the gardens of the monasteries of the Jesuits and Recollets and of the convent of the Ursuline nuns. Buade street refers to the Comte de Buade, Governor Frontenac. The name Sous-le-Fort street evokes the days when the Governor's fort, the Fort Saint-Louis, looked down on the Lower Town. Along with its winding streets, Quebec City is known for its staircases linking the Upper and Lower Towns. There are 28 of them in all. The best known is the Escalier Casse-cou or Breakneck Stairs.

Sainte-Anne street is one of the most picturesque in all of Quebec City.

Quebec City reveals its secrets only to those who visit it on foot.

◀ *Photograph
of pages 26 and 27 :
Lower Town
and Upper Town*

Anchored to the cliff overlooking the river, the boardwalk offers a spectacular, breathtaking view.

A very important discussion in the shadow of the cliff on Sous-le-Cap street.

The brightly colored roofs along Saint-Paul street.

The côte du Palais is a street that used to lead down to the Intendant's residence or "palais".

29

Where life is sweet and to be enjoyed.

Inside the Old City some of the most interesting sites include the terrace at the end of Saint-Denis street that overlooks the Dufferin Terrace and the Château Frontenac, or the rue des Remparts with its view of the Louise Basin, port and Laurentian Mountains, and the 31st floor of the Marie-Guyart building that offers a 360 degree view of the city and surroundings. Two other remarkable sights are the view of the city itself from the river or the heights of Lévis and the view from Sainte-Pétronille at the tip of the Ile d'Orléans.

Two walks offer special insights. One along the top of the city fortifications crosses over the city gates providing views inside and outside the old city. The second is easiest when begun on the boardwalk on the Plains of Abraham. Follow it down to the Dufferin Terrace. This offers an ideal view of the river from the Quebec Bridge to the Ile d'Orléans.

Within the walls of the Old City is found a wealth of architecture, conserved over four centuries and marked by the influence of both France and England. Sober merchants' houses from the eighteenth century contrast with the picturesque buildings of the Victorian era. The Parliament resembles the Louvre in Paris while the Price Building makes one think of the skyscrapers in New York in the 1920s and 30s.

The architecture of the famous Château Frontenac hotel is inspired by the chateaux of the Loire Valley in France. Visitors often ask why among the many colors to be seen, so many roofs in Old Quebec are green. This is due simply to the copper roofing that oxidizes over time acquiring a distinctive pale green patina.

Two streets in particular deserve mention: Saint-Paul near the Old Port lined with antique shops, galleries of modern and traditional art and the prestigious Grande Allée that one could call the Champs-Elysées of Quebec City which runs along the Parliament under superb elm trees.

Another neighborhood which deserves a visit, is the Faubourg Saint-Jean-Baptiste. A picturesque and lively quarter, it houses specialty shops, boutiques, and ethnic restaurants. The rue Saint-Jean, its main street, is now a delight for pedestrians.

The beauty of the city, recently named a World Heritage Site by UNESCO, is incalculable: multi-paned windows, richly carved door and window frames, porte-cochères, stone walls, forged iron locks, stone sidewalks. Anyone strolling will succumb to its subtle, yet striking charm.

Spring colors.

The Quebec International Summer Festival

The Quebec International Summer Festival is like no other. For over twenty five years this French-speaking expression of street and performing arts has been characterized by top quality entertainment, friendliness, openness and audacity. The Festival has large, open-air stage shows, as well as personal encounters with street performers, all part of its charm. Over a period of eleven days there are hundreds of shows put on by more than one thousand artists from dozens of countries. Song, performance art, world beat, classical music and street performers are all part of a festival program that includes a wide range of styles. The Festival is made for the streets of Old Quebec City and has to be experienced on foot. It is also the only international event of its kind that honors French-language performing artists with a major prize, the Prix de la chanson francophone. In July, Quebec City is the Summer Festival.

*A memorable moment
on Sainte-Ursule street.*

A Romantic City

The thousands of tourists who visit Quebec City throughout the year sing its praises in different ways. But the most common refrain that is heard is: It's so romantic... *Que c'est romantique*. The romance of Quebec City rivals that of Paris or Venice.

This is due first to its exceptional setting. Built on the promontory often called the Gibraltar of the North, Cape Diamond, Quebec City watches over the sea as if still waiting for the French and English tall sailing ships of old.

And this heritage is far from lost. It can be found inscribed in the stone homes, in the architecture so carefully maintained and in the streets that still follow their original path. Where many other cities have been forced to modernize, Quebec City has stubbornly refused facelifts or cosmetic changes.

To get a feel for forgotten moments of time, take a summer stroll through its numerous parks under the giant elms captured on canvas so lovingly by Marc-Aurèle Fortin. Walk through the shade of narrow streets lined with history, streets that take you up and down and zigzag slowly around to your destination. Enjoy a ride in a gaily decorated horse-drawn buggy while seeking out monuments and historic sites.

Something to discover wherever you look.

A breathtaking panorama.

Venture into one of the steep streets leading up from Lower Town or up the Breakneck stairs. On the Côte de la Montagne to the south there is a dizzying descent to the river past the roofs of the city square so aptly named Place Royale. This is where the first explorers and colonists landed, where the fur trade began and where Champlain, founder of the city, built his first dwelling. The cradle of New France.

Walk along the wharves to the ferryboat to Lévis. This short excursion on one of the world's great rivers offers you, for a moment, the same breathtaking view that made Jacques Cartier stop and land. Local sailors continue the tradition and there are dozens of sails on the river filled with the wind that never stops blowing in this valley headed to the sea.

L'Imagier / Christian Bibeau

Shadows and light.

Carved in stone and caressed by the river, Quebec City offers, to those who love it, a chance to relax in the warm atmosphere of its many French-style cafés savoring Québec hospitality with fine wine and renowned cuisine.

Visitors who know the city well, whether they come from Boston or Saint-Malo, often prefer to enjoy Quebec City in the fall. Then, the old city dramatically shoulders the onslaught of North Atlantic winds that rage on the river. There are moments when the city, whipped by the rain, falls into a somber, dramatic melancholy that would be appreciated by fans of Edgar Allen Poe or Alfred Hitchcock (who filmed I Confess with Montgomery Clift here). But all that is needed to warm the heart is to settle into one of the many comfortable, small family-style hotels in Old Quebec City and listen to the reassuring crackle of maple logs burning in the hearth. A home-style Québecois meal with a special friend would make the evening ideal.

In winter the white snow wraps the city in a mantle of silence. Few places in the city are more than five minutes from the Battlefields Park for a stroll or a cross-country ski excursion. From the top of the cliffs, the city disappears and the frozen river is barely kept open by the ice breakers. A breathtaking panorama.

If you are ready for excitement, try flying down the toboggan run on Dufferin Terrace next to the famous Château Frontenac. It is thrilling and it also offers one of the most beautiful views of the river, the Ile d'Orléans and the Laurentians on the horizon. There are few sites where the sky is so wide.

And then the first signs of spring after the ice breaks up. "Voilà les oies", "Here come the geese" in the words of songwriter and poet Félix Leclerc. Hundreds of thousands of wild geese winging their way north stop along the shores of Cap Tourmente and the Ile d'Orléans to regain their strength after migrating for weeks in flight. A spectacle that inspires inhabitants along the river with the wild freedom of the North.

At the same time, inside the city walls, the Rue du Trésor gets ready for summer. It attracts a great number of sightseers to one of the narrowest streets in the world. They come to enjoy the paintings and engravings of city scenes for sale hung along its walls. That is when Quebec City blooms anew. The sidewalk cafés open as people stroll by and romance returns.

When night falls.

An afternoon on the Plains of Abraham.

The City founded by Champlain is irresistible seen from Lévis.

Quebec City wrapped in a snowy mantle on a December evening.

Hotel or chateau ?

The Château Frontenac is to Quebec City what the Eiffel Tower is to Paris. The symbol of the city, its signature.

It was named in honor of Governor Frontenac, who was one of the most famous occupants of the Château Saint-Louis, the residence of the French and English governors until it was destroyed by fire in 1834.

At the end of the last century, Canadian financiers gave the capital a hotel worthy of the palaces of Europe. A romantic edifice, with round towers and cone-shaped roofs, it conceals a modern structure within.

From the day it opened in 1893, the Château Frontenac became the pride of the Canadian Pacific chain of hotels, although its distinctive 17-storey central tower wasn't completed until 1923.

In 1943 and 1944, Churchill, Roosevelt, Eisenhower, Mackenzie King and several other military leaders held the Quebec conferences in the hotel to plan the Normandy invasion of World War Two.

The Château Frontenac has been the host of many prestigious visitors such as Elizabeth II, Grace of Monaco, Richard Nixon, Ronald Reagan, François Mitterrand, Jacques Chirac and hundreds of personalities from around the world.

A fine meal in a one of the many sidewalk cafés, is another way to enjoy Quebec City's "joie de vivre."

A play of light. ▶

Indian summer.

In Harmony With The Seasons And With Nature

French poet Blaise Cendrars was surprised during a visit to Quebec City by the sudden and abrupt changes in springtime, such as the violent force of the ice break-up on the river when thousands of blocks of ice are torn loose. They strike the shores and city wharves and are tossed up and down the river by the tides. Sometimes huge blocks of ice are left stranded on the shore by the retreating tide.

Abrupt changes also happen in the fall with the arrival of Indian summer, a short period of warmth that interrupts the fall. It earned its name because it allowed the aboriginal inhabitants to lay in food one last time before the winter cold set in.

Quebec City, Snow Capital of the World.

A few weeks after the first cool weather, city dwellers who wore their light raincoats or carried their umbrellas to work can suddenly be surprised with ankle-deep snow on their way home. Winter arrives in one fell swoop and stays for five or six months. But on that first day of snow, a visitor would be surprised to find city inhabitants enjoying the spectacle. Their eyes shine in delight, their faces full of joy. The snow is so pretty and so clean - a bright white blanket covering the streets and the city. People in Quebec City feel at home with the snow. It's second nature. The first colonists did suffer during the winter of course. They even died from the cold due to the lack of a healthy diet or from diseases such as scurvy. The aboriginal inhabitants who knew of a remedy made from bark were not always present to help the European settlers. But the newcomers soon learned to prepare for winter, make warm clothes and build solid comfortable homes with steep roofs, small windows and large fireplaces. Some of these homes can still be seen in the narrow streets of Old Quebec City where they have remained almost unchanged.

Champlain, marveling at the beautiful site of Quebec City, called it a gift from the Almighty and his exclamation became part of the city's motto: "Gift of God, I will make thee worthy."

Snow removal is a "steady" job.

Winter fun.

Although at the same latitude as several major European capitals, Quebec City receives more snow than any other city... nearly four meters or 12 feet a year.

Hockey on the Ile d'Orléans.

The most photographed hotel in the world.

So winter is not just a struggle. It is the beauty of an urban, a rural and a mountainous landscape. It means winter sports such as cross-country or downhill skiing, hockey, skating, tobogganing, snowshoeing and sleigh or snowmobile rides. Visitors enjoy skating right in the heart of the city at Place d'Youville just outside the Saint Jean gates. There are three modern ski resorts only a fifteen to thirty-minute drive from downtown.

In late March or early April after several days of driving rain and high spring tides, the sun suddenly bursts through. Within just a week sometimes, the snow melts and the buds bloom on the elm, oak, maple and ash trees. While the sun warms the earth, tender leaves of fragile green clothe the city, hugging it closely. City inhabitants come out of their homes as if breaking a long silence to join bustling crowds on the sidewalks that have suddenly become very busy. Cars freshly cleaned of winter road salt slowly parade past outdoor cafés with tables set up in the sun...

Summer is a return to the easy life. The inhabitants of Quebec City love to stroll through their town and watch the river from the heights of Cap-aux-Diamants. They picnic on the Plains of Abraham or take in the sights along the city wharves or the Old Port.

Fall brings no regrets with its rich variety of color that transforms the numerous parks or streets like the Grande Allée and d'Auteuil into an Impressionist work of art. There are fewer visitors and the city takes the time to slow down and dream a bit before a new winter arrives.

Quebec City is a city built on a human scale that lives in harmony with its setting. Every season is enjoyed to the fullest.

Winter splendor on Saint Denis street.

Surprise ... for the first time this winter.

As soon as there is a hint of spring, city dwellers invade the
Plains of Abraham.

Skating at downtown Place d'Youville under the watchful gaze of Bonhomme Carnaval, the snowman host of the winter carnival.

Throughout the year the residents of Quebec City enjoy many cultural and popular activities.

CARNIVAL · CARNIVAL · CARNIVAL · CARNIVAL

The Quebec Winter Carnival... For a Warm Time In Winter

When winter envelops the Vieille Capitale, the city puts on its festive air, offering a unique and unforgettable spectacle. The Quebec Winter Carnival is one of the largest in the world and dazzles thousands of visitors with a wide range of activities. Quebec City turns into a festival and a cultural event as sculptors from around the world carve great blocks of snow bringing them to life and turning the city into an open air sculpture exhibit.

Carnival activities include an invigorating snow bath, the nighttime parades and the legendary canoe race with teams hauling their boats across ice floes and braving the current to cross the Saint Lawrence. It all happens in February in Quebec City. And during your visit you could meet Bonhomme Carnaval, the snowman host of the Carnival.

Set in flowering fields.

The Diversity Of Nature

From any part of the city, the mountains, river and countryside are always visible. Nature still untamed, remains within view and within reach. Ski slopes in winter and lakes for swimming are only minutes from the Old City. The romantic countryside of the Ile d'Orléans, famous in the songs of Felix Leclerc, is only twenty minutes away by car. Dozens of rivers, a multitude of lakes, endless forests with the temperature of Florida in summer and the Arctic in winter offer some of the greatest contrasts in the world and provide a variety of attractions and a wide range of activities.

At Donnaconna, just west of Quebec City, salmon ascend the tumultuous Jacques Cartier River using a migratory fish ladder. Further north, in the Jacques-Cartier Park, wolves howl and moose call. There is a herd of caribou in the Grands-Jardins Park only a two hour ride from the city. A little further on, near Tadoussac, blue whales, finbacks and other whales make their annual trek. They can be observed close at hand from small boats.

Hunting and fishing are not the only sports. Within a short distance it is possible to go canoeing on lakes and rivers, white water rafting or kayaking, mountain biking, hiking or deltaplaning. The Beauport beach, only five minutes from the center of the city, is popular for windsurfing.

All along the Beaupré coast there are waterfalls and rapids cascading down the steep cliffs, each one rivaling the next for beauty. Take a ride up the Montmorency Falls in a cable car. The Sainte-Anne Falls plunge deep into a canyon. The Jean-Larose Falls are in the Mont-Sainte-Anne Park and close to the spectacular Sept-Chutes. The Beaupré Coast that extends into the Charlevoix region is so known for its beauty that it has even inspired its own school of painters, the Charlevoix School.

Every winter the area at the bottom of the falls is transformed into a playground of activity.

The "sugarcone", an enormous frozen ice formation created over the falls by the intense winter cold .

Over a hundred feet higher than Niagara, the Montmorency Falls change dramatically with the seasons.

For outdoor enthusiasts, there are marked trails around the mountains, lakes and rivers just outside the city.

Tourisme Québec

Area ski stations offer night skiing with some of the best snow ever.

Jean Sylvain

Tourisme Québec

Moose are just one of the many species that inhabit the immense Laurentian forest.

In addition to the many parks and nature reserves, the area surrounding Quebec City offers many natural attractions, such as the Stoneham Tourist Center, the Village des Sports and the Jacques-Cartier Park.

Special attractions near the city include Wendake, a Huron community which is the most urbanized Indian Reserve in Canada. The Basilica of Sainte-Anne in Beaupré is only a half-hour pilgrimage from Quebec City. There are over 1 200 000 visitors to this pilgrimage site every year.

Two other major regions border the Quebec City area: south of the Saint Lawrence, the Chaudière-Appalaches region that is easily visited by ferry or by crossing one of the two bridges and the Portneuf area to the west that offers all the attractions of the countryside along with the savage beauty of trackless forest and mountain landscapes.

Nature with its many facets is alive in Québec, easily accessible and part of the fun, recreation and sports activities.

Michel Harvey

A trip around the Ile d'Orléans takes visitors 350 years back into a rural tradition that is still intact.

Fields of dreams.

There are a wide range of outdoor activities available in the Jacques Cartier Valley including canoeing slowly past magnificent scenery.

A morning scene in the fall at Neuville near Quebec City.

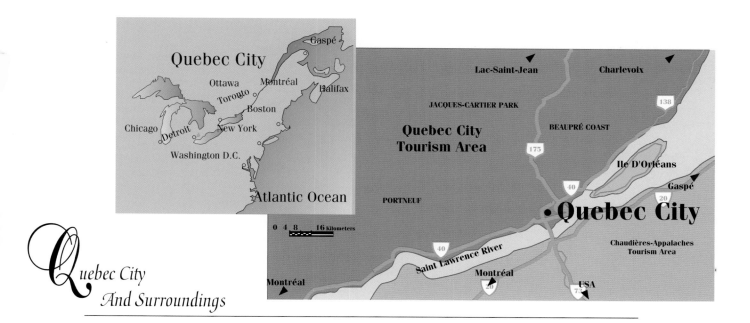

Quebec City And Surroundings

Quebec City is the capital of the Province of Québec, the largest province in Canada. The metropolitan area has 670 000 residents and takes 13 064 square kilometers, an area the size of the State of Connecticut, twice that of the Province of Prince Edward Island or almost half the size of Belgium. Old Quebec City covers half a square mile with no less than 3000 buildings including the Citadel and several large, historic institutions.

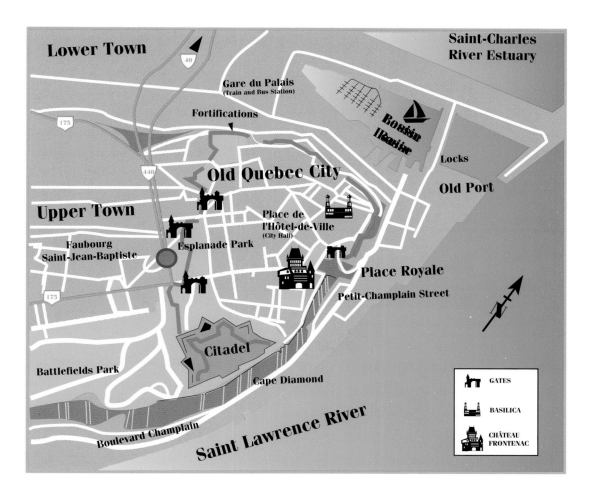

Luc-Antoine Couturier, an artist working in images and light, has a personal vision that captures special shades of life. Fortunately for us he has chosen Quebec City as his inspiration. His sensitive and unobtrusive approach reveals the heart of Quebec City along with glimpses of unsuspected facets of this marvelous city.

Epilogue

According to Louis-Guy Lemieux, a columnist at Quebec City the daily, Le Soleil, Quebec City is one of those rare cities that does not belong just to its residents. Like Paris. Like Rome. Like Florence... We could add that Quebec City reveals itself to those who take the time to get to know it...and who succumb to its charm.

We hope that this book will help you discover and appreciate Quebec City and lead to many years of exploring the city and its surroundings.

ILLUSTRATIONS :

Page 8 : The illustration : The Quebec City area from the Ice Age to Today is inspired by a Master's thesis from François Morneau published by the geography department of Laval University in 1986.

Page 8 : The illustration : The Quebec City area in the 16th Century is inspired by a book by Marcel Trudel. Initiation à la Nouvelle-France. Histoires et Institutions. Montréal, Holt, Rinehart et Winston ltd., 1968.

PLATES :

Page 9 : Late 18th century Huron porcupine quill decoration from Lorette. Here the heart, symbolic for Europeans, is treated as part of a geometric design. Collection. Musée de l'Hôtel-Dieu, Québec. L'art traditionnel au Québec. Éditions de l'homme. 1975.

Page 9 : Peace treaty, 1701. Ideograms representing the totem animals of aboriginal tribal leaders who signed a preliminary peace treaty with the governor of New France in 1700. © Archives Nationales - Fonds des colonies.

Page 15 : Abitation de Qvebecq. Woodcut from a drawing by Champlain for Les Voyages du Sieur de Champlain. Paris, 1963.

Page 22 : The ice bridge between Lévis and Quebec City. From a stereoscopic photograph by Louis-Prudent-Vallée. March 1892. Archives nationales du Québec in Quebec City, Fonds Louis-Prudent-Vallée, reference N83-11-9.

Page 38 : Neige dans les rues de Québec en mars (Snow in the streets of Quebec City in March). From a stereoscopic photograph by Louis-Prudent-Vallée, c. 1880. Author's collection.

Page 49 : Maps. O.T.C.C.U.Q.

For more information on the Quebec City region, please contact :

Québec City & Area Tourism and Convention Bureau

www.quebecregion.com